The Right Mistakes

Poems on
Imperfection and Renewal

The Right Mistakes

Poems On
Imperfection and Renewal

by
Pamela Brothers Denyes

© 2022 Pamela Brothers Denyes. All rights reserved.
This material may not be reproduced in any form, published,
reprinted, recorded, performed, broadcast,
rewritten or redistributed without
the explicit permission of Pamela Brothers Denyes.
All such actions are strictly prohibited by law.

Cover image by Pamela Brothers Denyes
Author photo by Pamela Brothers Denyes

ISBN: 978-1-63980-163-3

Kelsay Books
502 South 1040 East, A-119
American Fork, Utah 84003
Kelsaybooks.com

For my beloved family of origin
and the family chosen by my heart

Acknowledgments

Grateful acknowledgments are given to the following literary journals and anthologies where some of the poems in this book were first published:

A Tribute to Lord Byron: "Flesh Gone Missing"

Adult Children Anthology: "You May Not Know…"

Barstow & Grand V: "Corn Silk Flying"

Childhood, Volume I: "Both," "Twisted Tree"

City of Light: "Monuments"

Dreamstones of Summer: "Ontario Summer Porch"

Faith, Volume I: "All the Faiths of Abraham," "Redeemed"

Fauxmoir Literary Magazine: "Searching Remembered Rooms"

Field of Black Roses: "As I Lay Dreaming"

Friends & Friendship, Volume I: "Hand-written Note"

Held: "Openness"

I Have a Dream: "Safe in My Running"

Journal of the Virginia Writers Club, Spring 2021: "Arid Surface," "Evening on the Avenue," "Mrs. Creekmore's May Peas," "Trimming for Strength," "Dreams of the Edge"

Journal of the Virginia Writers Club, Summer 2021: "Releasing"

MindFull Magazine: "Carry You with Me," "Just This Once"

Poetry for Ukraine: "A Blue and Yellow Flag"

Poetry Virginia: Journal of Annual Contest Awards: "Explode like Lightning Striking"

Quilted Poems: "Frosty Forest Soldiers"

Tangled Locks Journal: "A Poet's Online Dating Profile"

The Poet Magazine: "What I'm Going to Do When Covid is Over"

Vanish in Poetry: "The Helper"

Wondrous World: Poems that Spark Magic: "Amber Eyes"

Contents

Honest as Open Wind	15
Renewal	16
The Right Mistakes	17
Listen	18
de·sire	19
Hand-Written Note	20
Casting Stones	21
Dreams of the Edge	22
Trimming for Strength	23
Cantus!	24
Concerto for a Mara	25
Searching Remembered Rooms	26
My Own Rosary	27
Mrs. Creekmore's May Peas	28
As I Lay Dreaming	30
There Must Be Wild Places!	31
Innocently Angry	32
Twisted Tree	33
Both	34
Acceptably Beautiful	35
Corn Silk Flying	36
Carry a Plant	37
Arid Surface	38
You May Not Know…	39
À Vendre	41
Evening on the Avenue	42
Ontario Summer Porch	43
Just This Once	44
Carry You with Me	46
The Helper	47
Openness	48
For a Hand in Mine	49

The Mystery	50
Amber Eyes	51
A Poet's Online Dating Profile	52
No Rigid Edges	54
Explode like Lightning Striking	55
Searching for Something He's Lost	56
What to Carry with You	57
Monuments	58
Flesh Gone Missing	60
What I'm Going to Do When COVID is Over	61
Rising from Pandemic	62
A Blue and Yellow Flag	63
Separating the Bleeding Things	64
Scaffolding	65
Blow Out All the Candles	66
Releasing	67
The April Planters	68
Frosty Forest Soldiers	69
Finding Something	70
Peace Lesson	71
All the Faiths of Abraham	72
Redeemed	73
I Have Forgotten to Care	74
Also My Unbreathing	75
The Sum of Our Choices	76
Savor All of It	77
To Be Mindful	78

Preface

I am that odd bird who enjoys reading history, even biographies. In reading about President Thomas Jefferson and his friend, Benjamin Franklin, I found that both men kept personal journals, as did many men and women of their era, which outlined their efforts to continue their personal growth in ways they felt important to an enlightened and developed adult's life.

Reviewing these lists of positive personal traits and habits, I found myself wondering which of them I might find still relevant. Knowing that April of 2020 would be a time away from all social activities due to COVID-19, I planned a National Poetry Month project to write poems on themes I found in these gentlemen's writings. Before it was done, I added several of my own, and when completed, the collection won an honorable mention in a Poetry Month competition.

As both Jefferson and Franklin acknowledged, this world spins us onward so swiftly, caught up in going and doing and loving, until we do not recognize ourselves as who we thought we wished to be. Allow these poems, full of questions, to slow you in your orbit long enough to reenter your personal and authentic path.

Enjoy! Pamela

Honest as Open Wind

Naked and free,
honest as open wind
visibly rippling miles
of supple prairie grasses,

stripped to purest snow,
white like a tiny seed,
a blossom fallen to the
solid warm soil beneath,

simple as the first
words you remember
from your child's mind,
I will speak from there.

What will you hear?

Renewal

For these aspects of me require
examination and renewal:

Impatience that will not hear a friend
rail on in painful negativity…again;

This mind that creates a life
more of fantasy than reality;

Restlessness as though I have something
awful to hide or to run away from;

Slothfulness—no, distracted focus,
attending to the easy things first;

Balance between water and wine,
sweets and beans, together and alone;

An internal life so rich that others
may not approach without invitation;

No reference point for allowing you
to be you and not in lock-step with me;

Faulty judgment from not hearing your truth
unfiltered when you tell me who you are;

Optimism that is assured largely because
I am adept at changing my requirements.

The Right Mistakes

To remember Thelonious Monk

I have decided
that I want to know
the lyrical patterns
which invite good things
into my one life,

to grasp them so well
that I can sit in
with any group of people
trusting that I will play
the right notes,

will make the right mistakes,
be the truest me, can riff
in delighted soul-filled
improv and be honest
with my own voice,

not crushing the melody
nor bouncing off-key
but for that accentuating
skip-note as I roll through
my moment in the lead.

Listen

Because all my life's answers
call to me from the woods,
I walk here and listen…to everything.

I watch for shifts and shapes, for light
to change, for some honest meaning
to make life clearer, breathing easier.

Today fog descends, shrouding the trees,
my view, cooling the fragrant blossoms.
Even the birds sing out to welcome it.

No wind will move this cloud mass
until day break, so I walk on in the damp
over-layer closing in swiftly, listening.

Moist fog has its virtues, after all.
I breathe in the mist deeply, releasing
my desire to escape its gentle wrap.

Birds call to each other until the very last
moment of the fog's incoming creep,
chirping and feeding in soft grayness.

Finally the fog, thick as cream soup,
overwhelms the woods. Even the birds
are silent again, and all is still.

What answer did I hear?
I don't remember the question!

de·sire

> : to long for, wish for or hope for
> some person or thing not yet
> in one's possession

It seeps away and flows
down to the basement
where I store boxed up
resentment, anger,
all my old feelings.

It dreams quietly there
in the dark underground,
waiting to wrap me like
a warm blanket when I open
the door and turn on the light.

When aroused, sleepy desire
remembers only the good parts
of loving another, without clinging
tightly to the difficult bits
or the inconsolable pain.

Hand-Written Note

A friend sent a hand-made card, with a
hand-written note, with the new stamp
commemorating my favorite garden.
Social distancing beautifully accomplished.

I miss our walks with lunch, delicious
specialty desserts split for two spoons.
Her husband has a life-altering disease,
which has also altered their relationship.

Several times I've thought she was ready
to watch him leave as he says he wants to,
to go to Utah, to die near his only son.
She's okay with that and so am I.

But he's still with her, here in Virginia,
where we're all on pandemic alert,
staying put until it's safe to travel again.
She did not mention him in her note.

Casting Stones

To those who would stone me
because you believe you are righteous
and I am not—

I ask you to search your mind
for some deep need, a hungry desire
beyond your rightful reaching,

Then see my own thirst in fresh light,
new understanding, also connecting
to the holy, and stone me not.

Go home to your lives in peace.

Dreams of the Edge

Spring, with her moody beauty,
with her quicksilver stormy weather,
dreamed of hot dry days, puffy clouds,
dancing nights as light as a feather.

Summer, arid without a drop, first
could not sleep for incessant heat,
then in exhaustion, dreamed of autumn,
himself prostrate at her chilly feet.

Autumn flowed with gentler winds
and rain enough for harvest's best,
but in her secret dreams one night
was shown she needed winter's rest.

Winter rose with a roaring chill,
blasting away warm harvest days.
One long harsh night he secretly dreamed
of warming green, of sweet spring's ways.

And so we dreamers will view this life,
each edge a welcome season's change,
through storms, arid heat, bounty and rest.
That, no elegant wisdom can rearrange.

Trimming for Strength

Outside my picture window, old trees sway,
April leaves fluttering dark-pale-dark green
in the spring-scented gale.

One tree was topped last week in a similar
blow; pathway blocked for several days.
It was a weak tree with top-heavy growth.

I get that way, too, all new sprouts with
little focus on the core of me, too much
in my head with no balance.

Then something in me topples and I must
pay attention to what stabilizes me,
what strengthens and grows me.

I must rest more or perhaps work harder,
define the health of body or mind, or lightly
move on from what was once important.

Life is to be shaped carefully, regularly
trimmed by the owner, in a gentle dance
with any gods or guidelines one chooses.

Fertilize the roots of your tree of desire, trim
weak branches of body and psyche, and then
sway in the breeze, knowing you are strong.

Cantus!

On Rautavaara's Cantus Arcticus

Listening to the quiet space before the concert,

a piccolo gently finesses soft notes, teasing
my ear. Then arises the chortling of birdsong!

They sing out from many hidden speakers,
sound bouncing around the large auditorium
as if the creatures are whirling above our heads.

The musical twitter and chat rises in intensity.
Violins and flutes mimic their insistent calls,
as cello and deep bass voices bow the taut
connecting notes, becoming a wavering chord.

Soon I hear a loon, a heron, the overactive baseline
chirruping of a tidal marsh full of wild things.
All of it rises, swells and swirls together.

I push to the edge of my seat, feeling I am outside
under a purple-orange sunset, overhearing the throaty

evensong of a million birds and skillful orchestra.

Concerto for a Mara

The Shostakovich last night quaked, blistering
background music for a Mara. Concerto no. 1
in C minor for piano, trumpet and strings, opus 35,

so perfectly written that the piano's scherzo notes
and schizo rhythms pranced the stage fiendishly,
the orchestra a rolling black ocean beneath it.

A horn soloist tooted unexpected pronouncements
or held very long notes at the oddest moments,
disjointed but so very moving, as odd dreams can be.

It sat on my chest purring and broke my heart...

Searching Remembered Rooms

Free of myself, I wandered remembered rooms,
full of people I knew or loved, or still love, amazed
to find them there, jamming together in a house I

once owned, or maybe two houses, morphed for vague
subject matter relevance, until there was just one house
with blended purposes and memories all mashed up until I

could not decipher persons or the ways I had known them.
Nor did it matter that I could not, for everyone was happy
to be playing music together. Noticing your absence, I

floated through all the rooms, the yard, to the river's edge,
searching for you, my long ago music man. Accepting
that you weren't coming, sad-but-angry tears woke me.

My Own Rosary

> For Juan Romero

June 5, 1968:
Yes, everybody's okay, sir, I lied,
feeling his warm blood flooding
my hand under his head.

Remembering we were both Catholics,
I pulled out my own rosary, wrapped it
around his right hand, with a little prayer
in my heart as they took him away.

For so many years I wondered what else I
could have done to keep this senator alive, he,
who worked so hard for low-income workers,
immigrants, the disadvantaged.

Why didn't I get the bullet intended for the good man?

Finally, standing at his grave after forty-seven years,
wearing the only suit I have ever owned, I asked
his forgiveness and breathed hard as very old tears
flowed like rain onto my new shirt.

Mrs. Creekmore's May Peas

Stormed hard this morning
after that tragedy yesterday where
anger boiled and two guns killed
twelve, a first in my home town.

Not sure Mrs. Creekmore had the
May peas I wanted, but she did. I know
when I go there that she will sell me
whatever's going to be on my stove tonight.

Mrs. Creekmore and I didn't speak of it,
the nearby slaughter, only pretty peas, red
potatoes for my pot, and strong young
onions, thinned from her garden.

Home from the farmer's market,
I shelled peas in silence and in pain.
Shelling peas gives you time,
time enough to think about yesterday.

Sweet May peas fell from my fingers
as I released them from sturdy pods,
gently freeing them, so as not to bruise
nor break nor bleed nor kill.

What unspoken ugly pain wracked this
killer of twelve co-workers?
Why did no one notice his anger,
so crazy it erupted in unholy murder?

Surely this sick man's murderous spree was
not about work, but about fear and anger.
Can't we be mindful of each other's pain
and choose to ask the hard questions?

I went to Mrs. Creekmore's again today.
She had mama and all her sisters there, and
somebody's husband, all together, keeping
each other close, like peas safe in a pod.

As I Lay Dreaming

As I lay dreaming,
someone read a poem aloud,
about a family without anything at all.

Even their cherished home country
was not theirs anymore, lost
to greedy wars and famine.

My co-creating brain painted
a writhing blue-red ocean, raging
and roaring with human sorrows.

This gigantic emotion-wave of many
millions suffering crashed down upon
my still sleeping body,

flooding salty tears to my eyes
and the iron taste of blood
into my mouth.

There Must Be Wild Places!

Sap like a black-water creek seeps
slowly through dry November limbs.

A garnet sunset shows through paper-thin
leaves, turning color now and glowing.

Still shallows glisten red-yellow-orange
with topsy-turvy images of transition.

A barely moving young snake hides out
under my terra cotta sculpture for warmth.

Feeder ledges are full of tiny birds until
bright cardinals and jays squawk to the tray.

Owl calls for a mate and hears prospects
returning her call from every direction.

Fox will have claimed her den by now,
and found a mate to help her fill it.

Someone said the eagle pair has returned
and begun to carry sticks high into trees.

Gratitude fills me because these wild lives
continue to thrive in my city, as it must be!

Innocently Angry

Oh, my little-girl self,
so innocently angry always,
teach me what to say about you,

help me to use honest words
that are the nearest to yours,

so we both may heal.

Twisted Tree

Deep in my sense memories, a twisted tree remains,
though long ago it fell to a city's progress.
I fled from home to visit often as a child.

Sandy dunes rose behind the ancient tree,
too hot on young bare feet, so I shinnied
up the rough low branches.

From the top I could see the blue-green ocean,
and on the land side, my empty house, waiting.
Nobody knew where I ran off to.

There, listening to happy bird songs,
the ocean's hypnotic thrum upon the shore,
my mind became still and free.

Years have erased the painful reasons
for my visits to the twisted tree,
like a wave smooths over a gull's tracks.

As I imagine visiting my twisted tree,
a simple warm peace returns, bestowing
the soothing mercies that time brings.

Both

Daddy's little boy and Mama's baby girl,
I was obligated at birth to be both.
There would be no more.

No one hungrily sharing my room
or following me to the twisted tree, and
no pesky sisters like my cousins had.

So eagerly I hiked with Daddy,
through sandy dune and snowy park,
tracking animals and birds.

Weekly I sat with Mama at the Beautiful Parlor,
terrified by the stinky tortures she endured
to feel acceptably beautiful.

Never interested in this curious female adventure,
I felt Mama's
ultimate disappointment.

Though he knew I could not be his little boy long,
I felt Daddy's
unconditional approval.

Acceptably Beautiful

Acceptably beautiful…
what a loaded phrase!

Hours spent, money invested
in a shallow, mercurial image,
hiding the truth of a person,
washing away the reality,

is not what I want for me, nor
what you should ask of me.
As you reach for my hand,
only the love in me shines…

acceptably beautiful.

Corn Silk Flying

I had a scary thought late today,
that my first husband had
passed away suddenly and
that was why my grown son
was not home yet.

I didn't want to be alone,
if it was true. I don't know why.
Maybe because all those years
ago, I pledged my honest
young life to him.

Perhaps it made me think of
my own aging mortal body,
which I will someday shed
like corn silk flying as I
husk an ear of corn.

Whichever one passes first,
I suppose, will untie the cord
from the cold other side of life,
finally loosening the promises
that bound us all those years ago.

But he did not pass today, and I
shucked fresh corn for my supper.
Whatever bonds still hold us,
we are all eating dinner tonight,
just not in the same house.

Carry a Plant

"Carry a plant from home wherever you go,
so you always stay rooted to somewhere,"
suggests a wise old-country proverb.

To every home over many decades,
some green and blooming plants
have moved with me, inside and out.

I carry their life with me in planters
or bags or buckets to begin anew
wherever I plant me.

Eleven heavy boxes also move with me.
Gently, I carry them to each new home,
so that my history stays rooted with me.

These precious boxes hold roots and shoots
of my family's love, my holiday keepsakes,
still-blossoming memories of home.

Arid Surface

Floating terra cotta hills against
impossibly blue skies.

Adobe buildings—red, brown, tan—
bounded by succulent blooming cacti.

Trails so chokingly dusty a kerchief
covers my nose and mouth.

Arroyos crackled dry, I easily cross,
following the path of energy

that rises and resonates
from the earth's roiling core.

It pulls me deeper into it, into myself,
as I climb each sunset-pink hillside.

It amplifies feelings I brought with me
to this sacred Sedona mountain:

red-chili emotions buried shallow,
just beneath my own arid surface.

You May Not Know…

For Susan and for Mother

Our mother knitted sweaters, using difficult circular needles
    at the neck.
Our mother was a wonderful hostess, always matching the napkins
    with the plates. Everyone wanted to be at Margaret's parties.
Our mother read books like a chain-smoker and played bridge
    like a master.
Our mother was steamrolled by the decision to leave you with your
    father and grandmother, but believed Nonni would care for
    you well.
Our mother was valedictorian of her class, then went to secretarial
    school because that was what poor smart girls did in the late
    thirties.

Our mother kept busy every minute of every day and compulsively
    made lists to be sure she got every large and little thing done.
Our mother was a weekend sun-worshipper, cooked to cocoa
    by August.
Our mother ate very little but smoked a lot, with gin in her Diet
    Fresca, and in everything else but coffee.
Our mother had her hair done after work every Friday, so she
    could feel acceptably beautiful on the weekend.
Our mother loved jazz and musical theater and took me to see
    all the stars.

Our mother was an executive secretary with mad skills, and kept
    the books for the all-male Rotary Club in the sixties.
Our mother loved you and missed you horribly, lighting up with
    joy when a letter came in or a long-distance call from you.
Our mother had a biting, cruel tongue that could cut you
    to the quick.
Our mother had different costume jewelry for every outfit, scarves
    for every sweater, and adorned herself with the latest fashions.
Our mother had amber eyes, nearly the color of beer,
    and handsome legs.

Our mother sang around the piano with my Dad and their friends, with her smoky alto voice. With any partner, she was a great dancer.
Our mother had cirrhosis at fifty and lived, then had butcher-knife dementia by fifty-two, probably earlier.
Our mother had constant burning leg pain, because she had phlebitis that kept her in the hospital for weeks after you were born.
Our mother had a philandering husband–my Dad. I doubt her marriage sanctity, too.

Our mother read the daily newspaper cover to cover, completing the crosswords in ink.
Our mother's father pointed a gun at her beautiful seven-year-old head, threatening to kill her if our Nana left him.
Our mother had a psychiatrist and a tailor because her life didn't fit her well.
Our mother made fabulous lemon meringue pies, with perfect crusts, but never ate them.
Our mother cursed, spat and told me she wished I'd never been born, as I drove her to the sanitarium one more time.

Our mother loved to meticulously decorate the outside of each Christmas gift, and every one had to be unique.
Our mother memorized "shaggy dog" jokes, the long ones with difficult punch lines, so she could entertain party guests.
Our mother was volatile like fire, calculating like a ruthless CEO, restless and constantly seeking approval like a seven-year-old.
I both loved our mother for being so beautiful and brilliant, and hated her for giving it all away to the things that destroyed her.

À Vendre

"For sale," the sign calls to me in French,
summer's lacy curtains barely veiling
ancient windows, neatly framed by honest
well-tended red geraniums.

At the crown of the house, the rooftop patio,
I'll sip my wine and watch this river's
temporary residents wondering who I am,
what riverside stories live here with me.

They won't know that I, too, wonder
who I am. What did I come here to find?
Perhaps to immerse or maybe to isolate,
to examine life through a lighter veil?

Ah, will I really move this far away, only
to observe myself in the unvarnished mirror
of French culture? To become another colorful
story in this apartment's history?

Evening on the Avenue

From inside a rented Haussmann apartment
on swanky Avenue de la Bourdonnais,
the Eiffel Tower is visible, but just the top,
as it is one block plus a park away. Each hot day
I walk the city, awkwardly gawking at landmarks.

From the corner Italian restaurant, richly herbed
tomato-based sauces and pizzas scent the air,
climbing to our third floor flat, which has all
windows open on this very warm late June day.
French wine flows as the first order of the evening.

Stepping over the French-door threshold onto the
small wrought iron-railed balcony, I watch two
proud long-aproned waiters below, smiling up at me.
They are selling tonight's specials in fair English,
then serving them in French to tourists like me.

Across the street, a lone saxophone rehearses.
Later, songs not in French or in English float up
the avenue from the restaurant closer to the Seine.
With my half-full glass and a Mona Lisa smile,
I am fully content absorbing life on this Paris avenue.

Ontario Summer Porch

French press steeping strong coffee,
I make a reading nest on the bright summer
porch of a large brick Victorian short-term
rental, guide books in hand.

For warmth, I pull the heavy woven
cotton throw from the stylish sofa.
It is the perfect weight for cool
southern Ontario mornings.

Lavender in white ceramic pots, centered
on the table, invite me to sit, so I do,
after retrieving my hot java from the
professional-cooks-only gas stove.

It's a tiny closed-in porch, with pristine
white chairs on a battleship grey floor,
framed by gleaming white tilt windows,
(which proved unreliable in a storm).

In Ontario for summer theatre, my photo
of that perfect seasonal porch, with the heavy
orange-red throw sends me back to the crisp
morning air. Doesn't the coffee smell good?

Just This Once

Just this once, I promise.
I will not look at it all
so closely again.

Eight years gone and only now
can I look up how your precious
brain was compromised by cancer.

Frontal lobes are social and sexual
behavior, initiation, impulse control,
spontaneity, problem solving,

motor control—that explains so much.
It must be why I could not get you out
the door for your last-chance treatments

near the end. Complex chains
of your thoughts and movement
disappeared, sometimes in a sad

cluster of effects. Almost no
facial expression, combined
confusingly with aphasia

and I had no way to understand
you, no matter how hard I tried,
and I tried untiringly.

You, the hearty quintessential creative
type, disappeared one brain-cell
at a time, until neither you nor I

knew who you were. A vanishing
brain robbed your decision-making,
precious memories, reasonable responses,

until your last hard-drawn breaths
closed out your remarkable
life's loving days.

I choose to remember the vibrant thinker,
planner, lover, father, husband, brother
you were in your sixty-three years.

Carry You with Me

I will not carry the astounding
grief of your illness, your sad
passing from our life together.
It is released, vanquished
from the storehouse of my
humble hopeful heart.

As you have passed beyond
the veil and I have not,
so every together-thought,
the travel plans, family dreams
yet have life to go forward,
if I will cease to grieve you.

Yes, I will wish you were here,
name your name in love always,
remember you to family,
to friends who treasured you
in your one magnificent life,
and forever carry you with me.

The Helper

From a distance I saw a glow around him.
He looked maybe seventy or so, with almost
translucent white hair, and like someone
I should know, but not entirely.

All of his loose-fitting clothing was white, too.
As he came nearer, I did not see wrinkles
in his skin, nor any flaw. I said hello
and asked his name.

"I used to have a name," he said, "but
it's gone now, and I don't really miss it."

>   Wait… did he actually *say* that
>   or did I just hear it?

The glow around him brightened
as I realized we were not speaking,
but communicating with each other
by pure intention.

I felt comfortable and warm,
as my own body began to glow.

Asking what he does, I heard only,
"I am a helper now, here to help you.
Relax and allow your life to be smoother.
Relax and allow… Relax and allow…"

I awoke feeling so very calm,
with just a little more glow than usual.

>   Was it you?

Openness

Listen…
all is still,

out beyond the thoughts,
above my mantra,

where there is honest breath
but I am not the one breathing.

There is a body but I
am not feeling it.

There is only openness,
free-floating comfort,

where I am I
and I am not I.

For a Hand in Mine

I would fly to the moon
to capture her moon beams,

Maybe go on through the luminous
universe collecting stardust for you,

Swim the teeming seas searching
for a just-right beach for love-making,

Sleep together in Tut's pyramid to hear
our loving words echo in ancient chambers,

Ride the back of a she-elephant across
the Alps to meet you in Rome,

Build a beautiful love-trap apartment
in Paris to intrigue and draw you in,

Become a master painter so I can
give eternity to your vigor,

Choose you every single day,
loving, uplifting and holding your hand.

The Mystery

What a mystery it is that love restores us again and again!
Though combat scars bleed, we seek another, better chance
to pour ourselves fully into loving another being.

Hurt places heal, bruised hearts feel stronger rhythm,
pumping sweet blind hope through still gaping wounds
from previous battles, and we feel love again.

This pulsing red hope, coursing through battle-worn bodies,
crosses the blood-brain barrier like no drug ever will,
selectively erasing painful lessons and errors.

So new love appears not as a war but as a tasty mystery,
a bright joyful expedition of unexplored territory,
rich with exciting possibilities.

Pressing on toward expected rewards in a passionate
heart-driven conquest, in spite of ourselves
we are restored by love once again.

Amber Eyes

I never heard chants or spells
but folks thought my Mama
and her grandmother were
somehow queerer than other folk
in eastern North Carolina,
including Mama's amber eyes.

Mama was superstitious,
attributed to her grandmother
who had lived in their home,
reported to be half Lumbee or
Cherokee Indian, though it's
not showing up in my blood.

Mama went to the best local psychic,
who said that her amber eyes meant
something exceptional for her, not to
waste it. Given her problematic life,
I can only assume Mama ignored
the good psychic's advice.

My eyes are now ocean blue-green.
Though formerly blue like sky, now
they bubble with green and amber,
changing with mood or colors I wear,
unpredictably shifting, like the special
blood of my ancestors.

A Poet's Online Dating Profile

I smell like ginger, apples and caramel, and often garlic.
My voice is a magnolia blowing in a sea breeze.

I have hungry hands that demand to be held.
My tiny ears connect to my heart, not my brain.

I am soft and warm, except in the hurt places, where
I am dangerously sharp and wince at allowing newcomers.

My lips are raspberries with lemon zest.
My green-blue ocean eyes can rinse a soul clean.

I am a Water Dragon, born on the cusp of Virgo and Libra,
with the best and worst tendencies of both.

My mind is wordy, argues with me about what I want,
and is hard to put to bed, like a four-year-old.

I have a quirky smile with a mind of its own.
My body glides magnetically to a body I love.

I feel deeply and often give too much of me away.
My heart lives on my sleeve and tears may run down my arm.

I enjoy an orderly space and hate to clean, but I do it anyway.
My days are colorful, creative and conscientious.

My sons and grandkids are precious like water to me.
A vivid imagination gives me more life than I can ever live.

I can hide like a bandit and run away from what scares me,
and sometimes what scares me is actually good for me.

I struggle to remember that self-doubt is not a stop sign.
I must take a walk to lose a difficult mood or outright anger.

I am a positive-minded Pollyanna, with a little of Mary Poppins'
practical magic for good measure.

My emotions rule my body, so I keep them happy and healthy.
I light up like Christmas when the right person walks into a room.

My life has been busy, challenging, loving, giving, rarely boring,
and I can feel it beginning to slow down.

No Rigid Edges

To define myself
with rigid edges
is to lock in a path
that I may later
wish not to have
followed so firmly.

The very thing we
most strongly believe
ourselves to be,
eventually becomes
the hardest thing
we must ever escape.

Explode like Lightning Striking

Because we have so few trees now
but so many cell phones,
I saw a man lynched, murdered
under the knee of another man,
just another angry man.

The few trees and many mothers
cry out in remembrance, in
recognition of Cain slaying
Abel all over again. How many
can the crying mothers and the

all-seeing trees take inside
of their bodies before they
explode like lightning striking,
from anguish, pain of generations
of saplings, cut down in their prime?

Who can blame them?

Searching for Something He's Lost

I don't know him well but he's a writer like me.
A successful thirty years ahead in his career,
he thinks he's my age in his disappearing mind.

Sitting across from him at a mentoring brunch,
watching weathered Chesapeake Bay-blue eyes
searching for something he's lost, I listen and smile.

A basketball star, football hero, swims daily, stalked
for his "great sex" reputation, he won't remember
much of our conversation today, he warns me.

Where does a man's understanding of himself reside
when his brain no longer stores away anything
but ancient cherished memories of vanishing youth,

and his body won't do anything he remembers?

What to Carry with You

> For my grandchildren

No *thing* can go with you.
Carry the brightest thoughts,
irreplaceable loving feelings,
bright hope for the future
and the joyful sweetness
that is your youth.

Give away the rest, spend
yourself and those worldly
goods on the people you love,
and share some with those
who have little to build
a life on at all.

Let loving kindness be your honest
life's work. Every big decision
is a choice between love and fear,
for they resolve always to these.
Choose love and it will be the spark
for success, lifting all your days.

Use your one life's energy for good,
for progress without pretension,
holding to love's instructions,
which you will always hear
if you keep your truest self
alive inside and out.

Monuments

Paris, the City of Light, glows in unholy firelight as
antique treasures burn, hallowed timbers becoming
torches, a hellish flickering furnace for smelting golden
Monuments.

Are the precious relics safe, the thirteenth-century windows?
A chain of human hands passes beloved artifacts to safety
beyond the viciously lapping flames chasing the cathedral's
Monuments.

Les Pompiers de Paris rehearse for such difficult tragedies.
Tonight they aim deluge guns, spewing Holy Seine Water
carefully over the blazing World Heritage Site's too-hot
Monuments.

Believers huddle together, crying and softly singing,
gazing longingly. Fearing great destruction they pray,
begging for mercy, for forgiveness from their Saints'
Monuments.

The cherished spire collapses, endangering les pompiers
and volunteers who, in their scorching spiritual zeal, are
compelled to offer themselves in service to the revered
Monuments.

In a fire so hot that lead in unforgettable windows melts,
can the pipe organ be saved to inspire a nation again?
Quiet statues, Apostles not at home, remain undamaged
Monuments.

Stone rib vaulting erected beneath ancient leaded-oak beams
miraculously protects the Sacred Altar, Tunic of St. Louis,
venerable Virgin of Paris, but sooty layers crown worshipped
Monuments.

As the ashes cool in Paris' golden dawn, we learn that
the repair, the rebuild, the recompense is already pledged,
penitent sacrifices from those who have made money their
Monuments.

Flesh Gone Missing

Surely this is the longest time
I have been without it—
no human touch for these many

months of longing loneliness,
tugging me through near-meaningless
days and still, purposeless nights.

To keep the ones I love safer,
I avoid touching them, as though
I am an infectious leper.

My aching soul feels every
missed hug is another piece
of my flesh gone missing.

Will I have any remaining
body parts when, at last,
we can hold each other again?

Will you recoil at the sight
of one so horribly disfigured
by the longing for your touch?

What I'm Going to Do When COVID is Over

Savor pad Thai and garlic vegetables
With savory friends, bringing home
Leftovers to last me for days.

Rock out with a live symphony orchestra,
My constant companions in lock-down,
Without fear of someone getting sick.

Venture out to meet new friends, adventures,
Perhaps someone special, which I have not
Desired until the seriously lonely times.

Invest my extra hours in any kind,
Loving volunteer work, anything I
Can do to make others' lives better.

Spend time, most importantly, with family…
Lots of time, with no more Zoomed holidays!
Lost time was the hardest loss of the year.

Rising from Pandemic

When the snake on the path has slithered
into underbrush, how alive and alert I feel!

Knowing the viper could easily have attacked,
I breathe deeply with its retreat.

Will it not be so, as we rise from pandemic
together, ready to thrive, still alive?

Aren't we alert now to the challenges
that could rob us of our very lives?

Won't we be less willing to throw away
somebody else's life for little reason?

Surely we're ready to embrace one world
of many colors, more valuable than gold.

So feel stronger now for lessons learned
and grateful for its slithering retreat.

A Blue and Yellow Flag

Exodus shifts a nation's people westward.
    With no peril involved, I drive westward from my home.
Afraid to run, a mother cannot find food for the children.
    In Virginia, a pair of finches pulls fluff for a spring nest.
Bodies queue up on the square, still in acrid smoky air.
    Here, a fly walks safely toward my coffee cup.
He's a famous American who had to walk to get out of Ukraine.
    Beyond my window, a deer walks, safely grazing.
Their president vows to stand and fight with his people.
    Today I will stand on a mountain's ledge praying for him.
Thirteen children killed by aggression, so far—war crimes!
    Fly lands on the glass door; I have no taste for killing today.
Russian troops hover like flies on a still-warm carcass.
    Raise the fly-swatter, Europe, and clear the air!
Everybody has a reason not to challenge a dictator.
    A hunting hawk circles above the mountain's tree line.
Democracy careens downward, nothing to stop it, save the bottom.
    Supportive sunflowers swarm social media.
Apartment buildings burn and crumble to the square.
    I will do more than fly a blue and yellow flag.

Separating the Bleeding Things

> She who loves must also learn how to organize pain.
> —Latorial Faison

She finds ways to file away awful hurt,
to deal with it some other day.

Her heart and mind ache from the bruising
of unrecognized trauma, but, no time for angst,

she separates bleeding things into I-can-help
and not-me/not-now. The latest scar-maker

enters, expecting her solace, but finds only
her lessons-learned triage system.

Scaffolding

Those challenging things
that happen as simple

Accidents

of a life scar and sculpt
and shape ugly bold

Wounds.

They work deep magic
for the woman who is

Unafraid

to feel the wound, massaging
scar after red raw scar until the

Strength

of them scaffolds to make her
more powerful than before.

Blow Out All the Candles

As a child, Chopin would blow out
all the candles and play in the dark.
What a teacher his piano had become!

My own deepest voice, the simple one
in my heart, speaks to me in the dark,
when I pause to listen carefully.

Driving down the road this voice comes.
I must pull over, for my eyes fall dark.
I am listening only to the words

of my inner witness. I do not hear
traffic, with my blood pounding dark
in my ears. Breathing grows shallow

until all is safely written down. I feel it
coming now—quiet, cool and dark—
so I will blow out all the candles…

Releasing

Center of a hot dry July,
not even coastal humidity
to soften the air, as just enough
southwest wind dries out
roots to treetops.

Floating brown pine needles,
too-early dried leaves fall.
As I breathe golden dusk
into tired lungs, sunset
slides down crusty trunks.

Rushing spring torrents fooled
garden and forest alike. Trees
burst with new growth, now
unsustainable. I mourn each
new branch or leaf gone.

A hidden voice whispers, "Let go,
so that you can make it through.
When hurricane season hits hard,
your roots will survive, if you can
release what doesn't serve you."

And release they do. First July's dry leaves,
then August's boughs, blown by storms,
hit the ground. September blows hardest,
challenging century-old root systems
to bite down hard and stay alive.

The April Planters

April's air compels me to put something into the ground.
To feed my young family from our own land, I tended
a full garden, with vegetables staggered in three plantings.

As little-uns, my three sons played and helped in our solid
summer garden, and ate fresh foods all season.
I still see little farm-tanned cowboys picking beans.

We drove to the U-pick farms, ripe with strawberries,
blueberries, bright scuppernong grapes with fat seeds.
Everyone came home stained with ripe delicious joy.

They have their own households now, and I hardly know
what they eat anymore, which feels so strange to me.
I will ask them whether they remember those gardens.

Today my sons' gardening grandfather, my dear Dad,
would have been ninety-three, and I have no doubt
he'd be sowing beets, with me right there helping him.

No, I'm not planting vegetables this year, but I will go
to local farm markets, buy fresh food from families
who still plant with the push of April's fresh air.

Frosty Forest Soldiers

I watched with quiet joy today
as the dawning winter sun danced,
glinting through frosty forest soldiers
rising silent and tall above the earth.

Shimmering sunrise rays, slanted in January's
reclining posture, shone briefly on each tree,
as though shining through a chilly thirty-foot
high slit in the day's busy schedule.

Warming light revealed the beech's speckles,
the old pine's woodpecker holes, shiny
still-green ivy rising from the dark thick
layer of autumn-tossed leaves.

Then, quick as the fox disappearing at dawn,
the fickle beam moved on and away,
as if to awaken from their winter sleep
another sleepy squadron of forest soldiers.

Finding Something

One red-bellied woodpecker comes.
She visits my winter feeders at least twice
every day, grazing on suet or seed.

Unlike other birds, she does not bring
her babes to feeders in early spring.
Rather, she teaches them to hunt bugs.

Like a man teaches his sons to hunt
but not where to find the easy life,
she gives them a taste for work.

As next autumn slips into snow cover,
the young birds will watch as she remembers
how to find something when there is nothing,

and they will learn that, too.

Peace Lesson

Some deeply internalized master teacher
lately brings me clever lessons disguised
in nearly every simple thing I do.

Today as I walked in a public garden, full
of honest wonder at the turning season, I felt
annoyed by constantly chattering youngsters.

I turned instead to the Japanese Garden, the most
reverently quiet space for me. Soon the gong there
reverberated under a child's eager hand and I heard,

"You must carry your own peace with you,
everywhere you go. Wear it like an unseen
garment that girds and protects you."

All the Faiths of Abraham

Dateline: Israel, 2021.
Twelve inches long, a forged iron key
opens the heavy wooden door of Jerusalem's
Church of the Holy Sepulchre each day.

By historical decree Saladin gave the key to
a loyal Muslim family, sworn to protect
the freedom of the multiple squabbling
Christian sects who worship there.

Christian monks, who still stand guard
inside overnight, are to this day locked in
and opened out every morning, by their
faithful Muslim brothers.

For all the faiths of Abraham
are brothers, are we not?

Redeemed

Into the pale mist
I send my mind,
to find the softest,
quietest faith on earth.

Away from all talk,
without colorful
distractions, my mind
empties itself at last.

This is my hymn, my
meditation, my honest
liturgy and joyful worship;
here, my humble offering.

Within this quietest faith
my confession is heard
and penitence accepted,
my tired soul redeemed.

I Have Forgotten to Care

I have forgotten to care about what I don't have anymore, the broken or missing, things that went out with the trash or to a new home. There are boxes never opened since my last move, with who knows what in them. I cannot waste a minute missing what I don't know awaits its unpacking.

I have forgotten to care that dust gathers as I am busy doing what gives me a joyful life, or adds to the lives of people whom I love deeply. It waits for me to scatter it like supple snowflakes. I have forgotten to care where I will put more books, multiplying like rabbits—pop-pop-pop!

The things, the people, the places that I have forgotten to care about are better gone than stealing time, energy, or attention from sweet memories that remain, precious images of beloved faces, mementoes of cherished places I hope always to preserve and to remember how much I care.

Also My Unbreathing

O, Central Essence of my Being,

within my breath
and also my unbreathing,

turn me always toward the future,
moving mostly forward, rarely back,

in gracious peace.

The Sum of Our Choices

Add them up, the big choices made
or perhaps not made. They all count here.

List them, subtract the losses, the heartaches
from your own less than careful choosing.

Find the flaws in your flawless options.
Grow your skill with sad hindsight.

Review current goals for strength, one by one,
and judge honestly which way to get there.

Life's unforgiving arithmetic eventually
proves us to be the sum of our choices.

Savor All of It

Taste it,
savor all of it.

Whatever you desire,
devour all of it deeply.

Relish the Monday morning
as much as Friday night.

This life offers ripe, juicy
fullness if you will seek

the whole adventure
that you alone crave.

You are the creative
designer of your life.

You get to decide what
to include, whom to deny.

Go and be and do
whoever you truly are.

Taste it,
savor all of it!

To Be Mindful

To feel the smoothness of the page
beneath my writing hand, and acknowledge
the handsome tree from which it came;

To hear the whole orchestra together
and yet be able to isolate and experience
just one instrument's delicious voice;

To walk a garden a thousand times,
noticing, appreciating every phase
of its honest natural progression;

To feel loving kindness for all the hands
that grew, harvested and prepared
the food I take in daily;

To listen, trying to be wholly present
with someone whose life is challenging
in ways I may never understand;

To observe the sun's rising and setting points,
accepting the constant progressive change
as a welcome companion;

To rejoice in the thousand greens of spring,
fully expecting later yellows, oranges and reds,
followed always by resting nakedness;

To watch my babes born, then theirs,
knowing it is all the same life essence,
showing up for a new generation's play;

To love another human being as myself,
and to serve, support, and gently walk
the wonders of this life together.

About the Author

Pamela's poems are published in various journals, *Wingless Dreamer, Vallum, Barstow & Grand V*, *MindFull Magazine*, and in several volumes of international collections published by *The Poet Magazine*. Her chapbook, "Renewal," upon which this collection is based, received an Honorable Mention in a 2020 National Poetry Writing Month Contest. In 2019 Pamela won the Hampton Roads Writers Conference Poetry Contest with her poem "Mrs. Creekmore's May Peas," about the mass shooting in Virginia Beach.

Pamela's career-based writing included contract nonfiction, instructional design and manuals, developmental and copy editing, and online/print writing for her regional newspaper and internet gateway. She is also a musician and singer, and has worked professionally in that arena, too. A mother and grandmother, Pamela resides in eastern Virginia but travels all she can.

Artist's Statement

Retired now, I am harvesting forty years of poetry, song-writing, journals and travelogues to create new works—and fun! I am inspired by creative arts of every stripe, and most especially the natural world. The brevity of form in poetry is the most immediately accessible type of art when that inspiration comes to me. A daily writer for a very long time, my affirmation is "May I never cease to be amazed!"